BRIGHT IDEA BOOKS

THE Truth ABOUT LIFE AS A YouTube Star

by Sarah Cords

CAPSTONE PRESS
a capstone imprint

Bright Ideas is published by Capstone Press, an imprint of Capstone.
1710 Roe Crest Drive
North Mankato, Minnesota 56003
www.capstonepub.com

Library of Congress Cataloging-in-Publication Data
Names: Cords, Sarah Statz, 1974- author.
Title: The truth about life as a YouTube star / by Sarah Cords.
Description: North Mankato, Minnesota : Capstone Press, 2020. | Series: The real scoop | Includes bibliographical references and index. | Audience: Grades 4-6
Identifiers: LCCN 2019029502 (print) | LCCN 2019029503 (ebook) | ISBN 9781543590715 (hardcover) | ISBN 9781543590722 (ebook)
Subjects: LCSH: YouTube (Electronic resource)—Juvenile literature. | Webcasting—Vocational guidance—Juvenile literature. | Bloggers—Juvenile literature.
Classification: LCC TK5105.8868.Y68 C67 2020 (print) | LCC TK5105.8868.Y68 (ebook) | DDC 302.23/4—dc23
LC record available at https://lccn.loc.gov/2019029502
LC ebook record available at https://lccn.loc.gov/2019029503

Photo Credits
Alamy: Birdie Thompson/AdMedia/ZUMA Wire/Alamy Live News, 11; AP Images: Amy Sussman/ZURU, 8–9, Stuart Ramson/Invision/Disney Consumer Products, 5; iStockphoto: Bhupi, 6–7, diego_cervo, 12–13, 28, JohnnyGreig, 20; Rex Features: Ricky Darko/BAFTA, 17; Shutterstock Images: Akkalak Aiempradit, 23, Alex Millauer, 26–27, Just dance, 31, Lightfield Studios, cover (camera), cover (boy), Shawn Goldberg, 14–15, 25, Syda Productions, 18–19
Design Elements: Shutterstock Images

Editorial Credits
Editor: Charly Haley; Designer: Laura Graphenteen; Production Specialist: Melissa Martin

Printed in the United States of America.
PA99

TABLE OF CONTENTS

CHAPTER 1

EVANTUBEHD

Evan opens a new Angry Birds toy. The birds are round and squishy. Evan uses a small plastic slingshot to launch them. He is having so much fun!

Evan from EvanTubeHD makes videos with lots of different toys.

Friends can watch YouTube
videos together.

Evan's dad films him playing with the toy. They post the video online to YouTube. Later the video might be watched more than 24 million times.

Sometimes Evan's sister is in his videos.

Evan is a big star on YouTube. His **channel** is called EvanTubeHD. He has made videos about toys and video games. He has even made videos about snacks.

FAMILY HELP

Evan's dad helps him make videos. They uploaded their first video in 2011. Evan was just 5 years old. Now 6 million people watch Evan's channel!

CHAPTER 2

BECOMING A
YouTube Star

Billions of people around the world watch YouTube. Many people also make YouTube videos. They post these videos to their own channels on the site. Most people do not become famous by posting videos online. But some YouTubers become big stars.

Dude Perfect is a group of YouTube stars known for their videos about sports.

POPULAR VIDEOS

The most popular YouTube videos are about things people really like. Many people enjoy videos about making things. They also like music videos or **clips** about video games.

Some people play music
in their YouTube videos.

YouTube star Angelique Cooper (right) took a photo with a fan.

Many **viewers** like YouTube stars who seem fun and truthful. People want to feel like they are friends with the YouTubers they watch.

CONNECTING WITH STARS

Sometimes fans send YouTube stars questions. The stars connect with their viewers by answering those questions in new videos. Fans get excited when they hear their questions in videos.

CHAPTER 3

THE LIFE OF A YouTube Star

Being a famous YouTuber can be great. YouTube stars often make videos about something they care about. YouTube lets them share this with people all over the world.

Some YouTube stars make a lot of money. But most do not. They make videos just for fun.

The British YouTuber DanTDM has one of the most popular YouTube channels in the world.

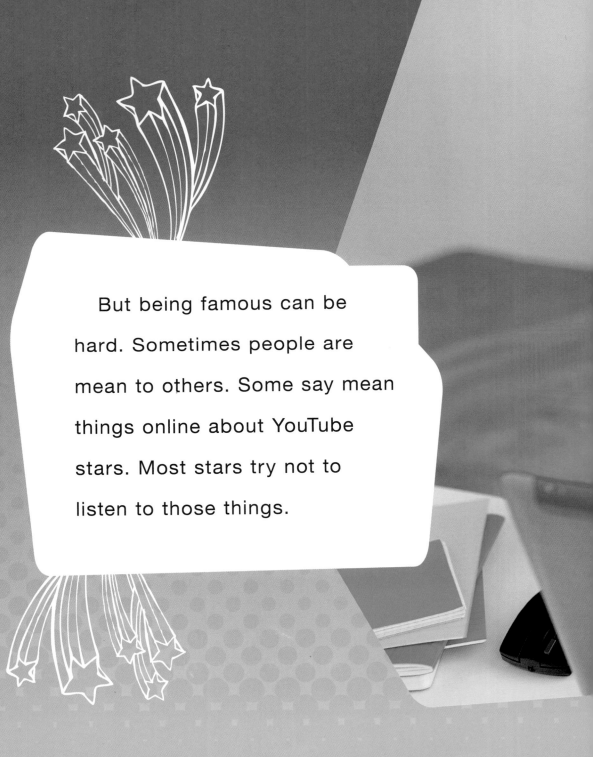

But being famous can be hard. Sometimes people are mean to others. Some say mean things online about YouTube stars. Most stars try not to listen to those things.

Any YouTuber can get
mean comments online.

Some YouTubers spend a lot of money on cameras and other things for their videos.

WORKING ON VIDEOS

Many popular YouTubers say it is a lot of work. It can take hours to make one video. Good equipment for making videos also costs money.

YOUTUBE CAMERAS

Anyone can make a video with their smartphone. But many YouTube stars use good cameras. A good camera can cost a lot of money.

YouTubers must also make a lot of videos. Fans always want to see new clips. Making so many videos can be **tiring**.

But many YouTube stars enjoy their work. They started making videos because they love it. They enjoy being famous for doing what they love.

Any YouTuber can get
tired of making videos.

CHAPTER 4

LIKE EVERYONE
Else

YouTube stars may seem different. But they are often just like everyone else. They like having fun. They like hanging out with friends.

YouTube stars
Akilah Obviously
(left) and Gunnarolla
talked at a festival.

Some YouTube stars are kids or teenagers. They do things other kids do. Evan from EvanTubeHD goes to school like other kids. He enjoys hanging out with friends. He also loves karate lessons.

YouTube stars are like other people. But their work stands out. They work hard to make great videos. Viewers like you make them successful.

YouTube star Colleen Ballinger, known online as Miranda Sings, started making videos when she was a college student.

channel
a YouTube user's account where they can post videos to the site

clip
a short video

tiring
making someone feel tired

viewer
a person who watches something

TRIVIA

1. **Ryan** from the YouTube channel Ryan ToysReview started making videos with his family when he was 3 years old. His videos show him playing with toys.

2. **Germán Garmendia** is a YouTube star from Chile. He has more than 39 million subscribers. He makes fun videos about things in daily life, such as making new friends or getting a job.

3. **Mariand Castrejón Castañeda**, who lives in Mexico, has a channel called Yuya. She talks about beauty and makeup.

4. **Carrie Anne Philbin** makes videos on a channel called Geek Gurl Diaries. She wants to teach other young people, especially girls, about math, technology, and science.

ACTIVITY

MAKE YOUR OWN YOUTUBE VIDEO

There are a lot of steps to making a video for YouTube. Try to do what YouTube stars do. First decide what you want your video to be about. It's best to choose a subject you are interested in or do well.

Next watch some YouTube videos on the subject you pick. What do you like about those videos? What should you do differently for your own video?

Then make a plan for what you want in your video. Write down two or three things you want to talk about or do. Do you need to gather anything to show or use in your video?

You can then record the video on a smartphone or camera. If you do not own one of these, see if you can borrow video equipment from the library or your school. After filming, watch the clip. Take notes for how you could make it better. Then, if you want, film it again. You can show the video to a friend or an adult. Do they have any ideas about how you can make your video the best it can be?

With an adult's permission, post your video to YouTube. Send a link to the video to your friends!

FURTHER RESOURCES

Interested in learning more about YouTube stars? Check out these books:

Kaji, Ryan. *Meet Ryan!* New York: Simon Spotlight, 2018.

Tashjian, Janet. *My Life as a YouTuber*. New York: Henry Holt and Company, 2018.

Watch This Book! Inside the World of YouTube Stars Ryan ToysReview, HobbyKidsTV, JillianTubeHD, and EvanTubeHD. New York: Simon Spotlight, 2018.

Interested in watching some popular YouTubers? Check out these channels online:

EvanTubeHD
https://www.youtube.com/user/EvanTubeHD

Mya, FullTimeKid
https://www.youtube.com/channel/UC0Grg2zrx1qlJtipR8_7GiQ

INDEX